They Fought for Freedom

WITHDRAWN

Nelson Mandela

Karin Pampallis

Series Editor: John Pampallis
Consulting Editor: Chris van Wyk

MASKEW MILLER
LONGMAN

Maskew Miller Longman (Pty) Ltd
Howard Drive, Pinelands, Cape Town

Offices in Johannesburg, Pinetown, Port Elizabeth, Kimberley,
King Williamstown, Pietersburg, Nelspruit, Bloemfontein and Mafikeng,
and representatives throughout Southern Africa.

First published 2000

ISBN 0 636 04329 0

Maps by John Hall
Set in 11 on 13 pt Sabon
Imagesetting and scanning by Cape Imaging Bureau (CT) CC, Cape Town
Printed by CTP Book Printers, Caxton Street, Parow

Acknowledgements
The author and publisher would like to thank the following organisations and
individuals for their assistance in the preparation of this book and for the use of
photographs and archival material: iAfrika Photos/Mike Hutchings, cover photo;
iAfrika Photos/Louise Gubb, page 58; PictureNET Africa/Jurgen Schadeberg, page
23; Mayibuye Centre and the Archives, pages 8, 28, 30, 33, 44; Robin Malan; Trace
Images, pages 64, 70.

Every effort has been made to trace the owners of copyright material, but in some
cases this has not been possible. The publisher would be glad to hear from any further
copyright holders so that appropriate arrangements can be made.

Other books in this series:

Contents

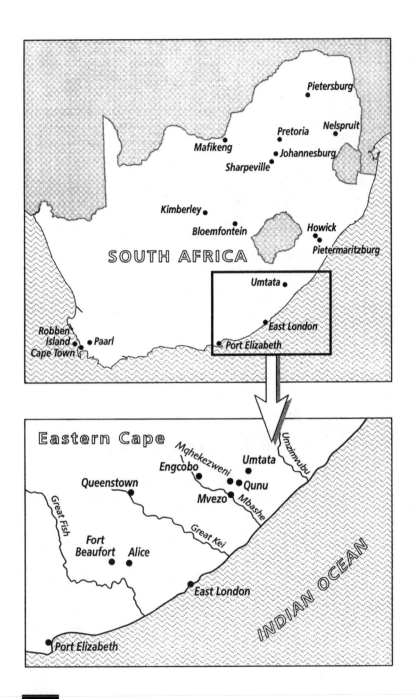

The 'troublemaker'

The boy ran across the grassy veld. He'd been herding cattle here for years, playing games with his friends. But after today he'd run here no more. Tomorrow he was off on a grand, frightening adventure. He was going away to his uncle's house, the Great House ...

* * *

The boy-child was born on 18 July 1918. He was his father's fourth son, and had nine sisters. His mother, Nosekeni, was the third of four wives. She lived in the tiny village of Mvezo on the banks of the Mbashe River, in the district of Umtata in the Transkei.

The boy's father was Henry Gadla Mphakanyiswa, a Thembu chief and a member of the Madiba clan. Tall, dark-skinned and with a proud posture, he belonged to the Left Hand House of the Thembus, the house which served as advisors to the king. He was also a member of the Transkeian Territories General Council. The Bunga, as it was called, advised the government in Pretoria on local matters, such as taxes and roads, and gave their opinions on laws affecting the people in the area.

'This child will be called Rolihlahla,' said his father when he first saw the boy. The name meant 'pulling the branch of a tree' but could be translated to mean 'troublemaker'.

A little while after Rolihlahla was born, his father had an argument with the local magistrate, an Englishman of great power in the area. As a result he lost his position as chief, and much of his wealth – cattle and land – was confiscated*. Nosekeni moved to Qunu, which was a larger village north of Mvezo. There she had relatives and friends who could help her. Rolihlahla's father visited regularly, dividing his time between his four wives as he had always done.

From the age of five, Rolihlahla spent his time herding cattle and sheep in the hills and valleys surrounding his village. He and the other herd-boys played stick-fighting. They stole wild honey from the bees and gathered fruit from the land. They swam and fished in the streams, and made clay models of animals. It was a life of wide spaces and freedom.

One of the things Rolihlahla loved best was to listen to the stories his parents told. His mother fed his imagination with Xhosa legends and fables. His father told stories of a different kind. He talked about times gone by, times before the white men had come to their land. These stories were very exciting, about brave warriors and great battles.

White people were not often seen by the boy at this time. The only ones he came across were the local magistrate, the shopkeeper from whom his mother bought tea, sugar and other supplies, and the occasional traveller through those parts. None of these people made much of a difference to Rolihlahla's life in Qunu.

When Rolihlahla was seven years old, his mother became a Christian. She arranged that her son was also baptised into the Wesleyan church. Although her husband continued to worship his ancestors and the Xhosa great spirit, Qamata, he did not mind Nosekeni's conversion. And when she came to him with the idea that Rolihlahla should be sent to the mission school, he agreed because he believed that the white man's education could be a useful thing to have.

The schoolhouse, just on the other side of the hill from Qunu village, had only one room where children of all ages learned their lessons. Rolihlahla gave up his traditional blanket for a pair of his father's trousers, cut down to fit him and tied around the waist with string. On his first day of school, he met his teacher, Miss Mdingane.

'Now that you are a Christian and going to school,' she said to him, 'you will need a Christian name. From now on you will be called Nelson.'

The mission school showed Nelson another world from the one he had learned about through the stories of his parents. There were no black heroes in the white history books. The books told about British kings and queens and explorers, British wars and discoveries, and British beliefs. They taught that everything British was good, and that other cultures were less important.

Nelson's father died when he was nine years old. After a formal period of mourning, Nelson's mother said to him, 'Pack your things. You are leaving Qunu.' His uncle, Jongintaba Dalindyebo, head of the Madiba clan, had offered to become his guardian. Jongintaba had decided that Nelson should join him at Mqhekezweni, the royal kraal.

When he left Qunu, the boy left behind a simple world to which he would never return. Time, age and education would wipe that world away.

A photograph of a village near Mvezo, taken in the 1980s.

2

The Great Place

The royal kraal was also known as the Great Place. Here Nelson did the things that were expected of boys his age – he ploughed, herded sheep, rode horses and played. In many ways, he continued the wild and free life that he had known as a herd-boy on the veld around Qunu.

Jongintaba's son, Justice, was four years older than Nelson. Although he attended boarding school, the two boys shared a hut when Justice came home for holidays. Nelson was nicknamed *Tatomkhulu* by his guardian and his wife, No-England; it meant Grandfather. 'When you are in a serious mood,' they teased, 'you look just like an old man!'

Nelson went to school in the one-room schoolhouse next to Jongintaba's house. He studied English, Xhosa, History and Geography. He listened to new words and strange names, and learned about far-away places.

Mqhekezweni was a Methodist mission station. It was more westernised than Qunu. Few people there wore the traditional blankets. Most of the men wore suits, and the women wore blouses and long skirts. There were more white people there than Nelson had seen in Qunu. Mostly they were traders who ran the few stores in the area, and government officials such as magistrates and policemen.

Nelson learned a lot about leadership from Jongintaba, who was regent* for the young Sabata. (Sabata was heir to the Thembu throne.) Nelson watched the way Jongintaba and the elders behaved in meetings. At the beginning of a meeting, the leader explained why the meeting was being held; then he listened quietly while everyone else had a chance to speak. At the end the leader summarised the meeting and expressed the consensus* that had been reached. If there was no consensus then another meeting would be held later to settle the matter.

> One of Jongintaba's favourite sayings was, 'A leader is like a shepherd. He stays behind the flock, letting the most nimble go on ahead, whereupon the others follow, not realising that all along they are being directed from behind.'

From the elders, Nelson heard many stories of heroes such as Sekhukhune, Moshoeshoe, Dingane, Bambatha, Hintsa and so on. He later wrote that he saw these men as '... African patriots who fought against Western domination. My imagination was fired by the glory of these African warriors.'

When Nelson was sixteen, he and Justice were prepared for circumcision*. This was not only a surgical act, but a very important ritual. The youngsters went to a special circumcision school for several weeks to prepare for manhood. Without the ritual and the ceremony, a youngster could not become a man. He could not own cattle or marry or take part in adult debates. The all-important operation was done by an *ingcibi*, an old man who was a circumcision expert. At the moment when the *ingcibi* used his razor-sharp assegai*, and pain shot through him, Nelson shouted the traditional phrase, '*Ndiyindoda!*' – 'I am a man!' During the ceremony, Nelson was given his circumcision name, Dalibhunga.

After the operation, the proud young men recovered in special circumcision lodges at a nearby river. Their bodies were painted with white ochre, made from a certain kind of stone pounded into a powder and mixed with water and fat. The white colour symbolised purity. After their wounds had healed, the young men washed away the white ochre and then coated themselves with red ochre, showing that they were now men. The circumcision lodges were burned and then there was a feast to welcome the new men to the community. Songs were sung, speeches were made, and gifts were given. Nelson received two heifers* and four sheep – he felt rich and important.

At some point during the celebration feast, Chief Meligqili made a speech. He began by saying how good it was to see that the tradition of circumcision was continuing, and how healthy and handsome the young men were. But then the chief talked about how the white people had taken control of everything. 'Now,' he said, 'these young men are slaves in their own country.'

Nelson listened carefully. What did the chief mean? Up until now, young Nelson had thought of white people as bringing good and useful things to Africa. He disagreed with the chief's speech, but it made him think. A seed had been sown in his mind.

After the initiation ceremonies, it was the usual custom for a marriage to be arranged. Jongintaba decided, however, that Nelson should be well-educated so that he could fulfil his destiny as counsellor to Sabata. The regent himself drove Nelson to Clarkebury Boarding Institute in Engcobo, where he began Standard 6 (Grade 8).

Higher education

Nelson spent two years at Clarkebury where he completed his Junior Certificate. He still believed then that he would be counsellor to the next Thembu king. As he was to say later, 'My roots were my destiny.'

When Nelson was nineteen years old, he joined Justice at Healdtown in Fort Beaufort, a town about 280 km southwest of Umtata. Healdtown was a mission school of the Methodist Church. It had about 1 000 students, both young men and women. Nelson was very impressed by the ivy-covered buildings and the big trees shading the courtyards where young students walked, talked and studied. He was also impressed by the principal, Dr Arthur Wellington, an Englishman who boasted that he was a descendant of the famous British general, the Duke of Wellington.

There were mostly Xhosa students at Healdtown, but also some from other cultures. Nelson made his first Sotho-speaking friend there, Zachariah Molete. He was amazed when his Sotho Zoology teacher married a Xhosa girl – marriages between different ethnic groups were very unusual in those days. Nelson gradually began to think about himself as an 'African' as well as a 'Xhosa'.

While he was at Healdtown, a friend, Locke Ndzamela, encouraged him to take up long-distance running. 'You're so thin and tall, Nelson,' said Locke. 'You have the perfect build for running.' Nelson found that he enjoyed the sport and did quite well at it. He didn't do so well at boxing though; he was still too light for it.

Mandela as a young boxer

In 1939, when Nelson was twenty-one years old, Jongintaba sent him to the University College of Fort Hare at Alice, about 30 km east of Healdtown. At that time, Fort Hare was the only university for black people in Southern Africa. Here Nelson met Kaiser Daliwonga Matanzima, then a third-year student. KD, as he was known, was officially Nelson's nephew, but was older and more senior to him. He took Nelson under his wing and they got along very well, although in later years they found themselves on opposite sides of the political fence.

In his first year at Fort Hare, Nelson studied the subjects of English, Anthropology, Politics, Native Administration and Roman Dutch Law. He had decided that he wanted to be an interpreter or a clerk in the Native Affairs Department – positions he thought were very important and influential. In his second year he took an interpreting course to help him with this aim.

He was active in sports, especially soccer and cross-country running. He also learned ballroom dancing; he and his friends spent hours practising in the school dining-hall. Nelson also became a member of the Students' Christian Association and taught Bible classes in neighbouring villages on Sundays. It was while doing this that he met Oliver Tambo, a serious young student who became a life-long friend.

One night, while Nelson and some other students were discussing the progress of the war (later known as World War 2) – they supported Britain's fight against the Nazis – a student named Nyathi Khongisa predicted that when the war ended English and Boer would join against the black people in South Africa, just as they had done in 1902 after the Boer War. This view seemed very radical to the other students, including Nelson. Nyathi was rumoured to be a member of the African National Congress. Nelson had heard of the organisation, but didn't know much about it.

During his second year at the university, in 1940, Nelson was nominated to stand for the Students' Representative Council (SRC). At that time, the Fort Hare students were protesting about the poor food served to them, and the SRC's lack of authority. As a result, the SRC elections were boycotted by most of the students. Nelson was one of six elected, but all six refused to accept the election on the grounds that the majority of students hadn't voted. The principal arranged another election the next day, in the dining- hall during meal time. This time, of course, nearly everyone was there and under the principal's watchful eye, another vote was taken. Although most of the students still refused to vote, the same six people were elected. Five of them then agreed to become the SRC representatives, but Nelson felt that because the majority of students still had not voted he could not take up the position. He refused to serve on the SRC, and was suspended.

'If you are willing to apologise and serve on the SRC,' the principal said, 'you can come back to Fort Hare next year.'

4

When Nelson returned to the Great Place, Jongintaba was very angry about his actions. He insisted that Nelson go back to Fort Hare, apologise to the principal and continue his studies. Nelson wasn't quite sure what he should do, but another matter soon made up his mind for him.

Justice, who had finished his schooling and was living in Cape Town, had recently come to Mqhekezweni for a holiday. A few weeks after Nelson's return from Fort Hare, Jongintaba called the two young men to him. 'My children,' he said seriously, 'I am not well and shall soon journey to the land of the ancestors.' Justice and Nelson looked at each other in surprise; they had no idea that the regent was so sick! He continued: 'Before I leave this world it is my duty to see my two sons settled. Therefore, I have arranged marriages for each of you.' The two young men were shocked. Jongintaba went on to tell them about the good matches he had made and informed them that lobola had already been paid. Everything had been properly arranged according to the Thembu tradition.

Nelson was horrified. He did not want to marry the girl the regent had chosen for him. He did not love her and he knew that she was in love with someone else. He believed in romance and wouldn't marry anyone he hadn't chosen for himself. Justice felt the same way. Nelson tried hard to persuade Jongintaba to cancel the arrangement, but the regent refused. Since he wouldn't agree to the regent's plans, Nelson felt that he could no longer stay at Mqhekezweni. The two impatient young men decided to run away to Johannesburg, eGoli, the city of gold.

Nelson and Justice waited until Jongintaba left on a business trip. Then they sold two of his best oxen to get some money for their journey.

They didn't have the travel documents that were needed by black people. They tried to get them in Queenstown with the help of Chief Mpondombini, a brother of the regent, by saying that Jongintaba had given them permission to go to Johannesburg. Mpondombini found out that they were lying and refused to help them.

Since they couldn't take the train without travel documents, they had to find another way to get to Johannesburg. They went to a friend, Sidney Nxu, to see if he could help them. Sidney told them that his boss's mother was driving to Johannesburg the very next day to visit her daughter. Maybe she would help them. She agreed to take the young men with her, but made them pay £15 for the ride. That used up nearly all the money they had, but they did get to eGoli, the city of lights and great hope.

When Nelson arrived in Johannesburg, he was twenty-three years old. He had lived in the countryside or in small towns all his life. He had lived a rather quiet and disciplined life, and he was well-respected as a member of the royal family. Now he was one of thousands thrown into the melting pot of this enormous city with its miles of streets and glowing lights, its cars, its tall buildings, its mines, its glamour.

That first night, Nelson and Justice slept on the floor of the servants' quarters in the house of the old lady's daughter. Early the next morning they went to Crown Mines. Some time before, Jongintaba had sent a message to the induna* there, Piliso, to tell him that Justice would be coming to Johannesburg and asking that a job be arranged for him. Now the young men managed to convince Piliso that the two of them were there on Jongintaba's orders, and that he should assign them work. Nelson became a night watchman, guarding the gate to the housing compound. Justice was given a job as a clerk.

'Gold-mining on the Witwatersrand was costly because the ore was low grade and deep under the earth. Only the presence of cheap labour in the form of thousands of Africans working long hours for little pay with no rights made gold-mining profitable for the mining houses – white-owned companies that became wealthy beyond the dreams of Croesus on the backs of the African people.'
– From *Long Walk to Freedom*, page 59

The two young men enjoyed their first days in the big city of gold. They were amazed by all of the new things they saw there, and were delighted that their brilliant escape had succeeded. They even boasted about how clever they were. That was a big mistake. A good induna knows everything that is going on among his workers, and Piliso was a very good induna. When he heard this bit of gossip, he decided to find out more about it. Soon he got a telegram from Jongintaba in the Transkei.

Piliso called Nelson and Justice to his office and showed them the telegram. 'SEND BOYS HOME AT ONCE!' it read. The induna was very angry. 'How could you have lied like this?' he fumed. 'Pack your things and get out of here!'

Well, they were certainly in trouble now – fired so soon after arriving in the city. But all was not lost. There were friends and relatives that they could turn to for help. Garlick Mbekeni, a cousin, lived in George Goch township south of Johannesburg. The two young men went to see him, and he agreed to help them.

Shortly after they arrived, Garlick said to Nelson, 'What are you looking for in Johannesburg? What do you want to do with your life?'

'Well, you know,' said Nelson, 'I think what I'd really like to do is become a lawyer.'

'In that case,' said Garlick, 'I know just the man who can help you.'

Garlick took Nelson to see Walter Sisulu, who ran an estate agency in Berkeley Arcade in the centre of Johannesburg. At that time it was still possible for Africans to own land in a few areas, such as Alexandra and Sophiatown.

Sisulu was a short, bespectacled man who had a habit of chewing his lip. He was also from the Transkei, but from a poorer background than Nelson. Self-educated, Sisulu was twenty-eight years old then, five years older than Nelson, but much more streetwise. He was to become Nelson's life-long friend and a great influence on him politically. But for the moment, what Nelson needed most was help in finding work.

When Nelson said that he wanted to be a lawyer, Sisulu helped arrange a job for him with a white lawyer, Lazar Sidelsky. At the firm of Witkin, Sidelsky and Eidelman, Nelson did a bit of everything – translation, running errands, and so on. The agreement was that he would complete his Bachelor of Arts (BA) degree by correspondence through UNISA, the University of South Africa, and then become an articled clerk* at the law firm. Nelson earned £2 per week. From this he had to pay for rent, transport, food, fees for his correspondence course, and candles to read and study by. Sometimes the money was not enough, and that year, for the first time in his life, he learned what it meant to be poor.

At his place of work, Nelson had his first close encounters with white people. Openly there was equality – for instance, they all had tea together. In reality, however, things were different – it was made clear that Nelson and the black messenger Gaur Radebe had to use separate tea-cups! Nelson chose not to have tea at all.

Nelson also met Nat Bregman, an articled clerk at the firm. Nat was the first communist* that Nelson ever met. Through Nat, Nelson met several other communists, and even attended a few Communist Party meetings out of curiosity.

At the end of 1941, the regent visited Johannesburg and asked to see Nelson. Nelson was nervous about the meeting. They had not seen each other since Nelson and Justice had run away from Mqhekezweni. But as it turned out, the meeting went quite well. Jongintaba was polite and caring, and asked about Nelson's studies and plans. It was clear that he no longer considered Nelson to be his responsibility. Nelson was glad that they had seen each other again, and that the disagreement between them was healed. He realised how important his Thembu heritage was to him.

A few months later, Jongintaba died. Nelson and Justice returned to Mqhekezweni for the funeral. While Justice stayed in Mqhekezweni to take on his new responsibilities as chief, Nelson discovered that while the Great Place was much the same, he had changed. He realised that he no longer wanted to be a civil servant or an interpreter, or even a counsellor to the Thembu king. His boundaries were now wider than Thembuland and the Transkei. His experiences in Johannesburg had opened new doors and given him different ambitions. He went back to Johannesburg a week later, convinced that his destiny lay there.

At work Nelson became closer to Gaur Radebe, who was a member of the African National Congress (ANC). The ANC had been founded in 1912, to give black people a voice in the newly formed Union of South Africa which had ignored the interests of black South Africans. Although the ANC didn't win equality for black people then, it continued to argue for more rights for black people. Nelson attended some ANC meetings with Gaur and listened carefully to the lively discussions about the pass laws*, increasing prices, and other subjects that affected the life and freedom of Africans.

At the end of 1942, when he was twenty-four years old, Nelson passed his final exams for the BA degree. He then enrolled at the University of the Witwatersrand to study part-time for a law degree. There he came into contact with white and Indian intellectuals of his own age, people who were to play a key role in his future – Joe Slovo, Ruth First, George Bizos, Bram Fischer, Tony O'Dowd, Harold Wolpe, Jules Browde, Ismail Meer, JN Singh, Ahmed Bhoola. He was impressed that these well-off young people were willing to work hard for a democratic government.

In August 1943, Nelson moved from being a watcher at the edge of politics to being a participant. He marched with Gaur and 10 000 others in the Alexandra bus boycott. The bus company had raised the fares from fourpence to fivepence a trip, and most people's very meagre earnings could not afford that. The boycott lasted for nine days and in the end the company reduced the fare to fourpence again. This experience showed Nelson how important the power of many people working together could be.

Nelson was much influenced by Walter Sisulu, who was politically active and a member of the ANC. He met other ANC members at Sisulu's home. By now, Nelson saw himself more as an African nationalist than as a Thembu or a Xhosa. He also began to see the ANC as an organisation through which Africans could fight for their rights.

Another person Nelson met at the Sisulus' was Evelyn Ntoko Mase, Walter's cousin. She was training as a nurse, as was Walter's new wife, Albertina. Nelson and Evelyn fell in love and were married in 1944. The couple lived in Orlando, first with Evelyn's relatives and later in a small house of their own. Together, they had four children: two sons – Madiba Thembekile (nicknamed Thembi) and Makgatho – and two daughters. The first daughter, Makaziwe, died when she was only nine months old; the second daughter was given the same name, to honour her spirit.

At the same time as the young family was establishing itself, Nelson continued working as an articled clerk and with his law studies at university. It was hard but he was determined to succeed.

5

Joining the movement

One of the people that Nelson met through Walter Sisulu was Anton Lembede. Lembede felt very strongly that Africans were wrong to believe the idea put forward by British colonialism* – that white people (especially British ones) were more civilised than black people. This ideology said that black Africans had to be led and taught by white people. Lembede believed that Africans were just as intelligent and worthwhile as white people. Africa was their continent, and they should not feel inferior to the people who were trying to take it away from them. 'The colour of my skin is beautiful,' he said, 'like the black soil of Mother Africa.' He felt that black people in South Africa should think of themselves as Africans first, and not as Xhosas or Sothos or Zulus. If Africans united, they would be strong enough to fight colonialism. Lembede's ideas came to be known as 'Africanism' or 'African nationalism'.

These ideas appealed to Nelson, as they did to a number of other young men. Up until then, the ANC leadership had been trying to get political equality for black people by sending delegations, petitions and letters to government ministers. It seemed to Nelson, Lembede and others that these tactics were not achieving anything. Thirty years after the founding of the ANC, black people still could not vote and had to carry passes, most could not own land, and many worked in low-paid jobs as labourers. Lembede and his friends thought that the ANC should mobilise lots of people to put pressure on the government. And African nationalism was the key to moving the masses.

The young men who were unhappy with the ANC's approach included Anton Lembede, AP Mda, Nelson Mandela, Walter Sisulu, Oliver Tambo, Lionel Majombozi and others. They decided that something had to be done to wake up the ANC leadership. Majombozi suggested that a Congress Youth League be formed to promote the idea of mass action, and to 'galvanise'* the ANC. The idea took root and in April 1944 about 200 people gathered in a hall in central Johannesburg to form the ANC Youth League. Anton Lembede was elected President, Oliver Tambo was chosen as Secretary, and Walter Sisulu Treasurer. Nelson was elected to the Executive Committee. Because the Youth League was considered to be part of the ANC, Nelson's membership in the Youth League meant that he also became an ANC member.

Nelson was strongly anti-communist at this time. Partly this was because of his religious beliefs. Partly it was because the Youth League felt that communism was a 'foreign ideology' which would not be of any use in South Africa. Nelson was also anti-white, and believed that co-operation with either white people or communists would not help the struggle for African liberation. He thought that Africans should unite and work for themselves, rather than be led by others.

'We believe that the national liberation of Africans will be achieved by Africans themselves ... The Congress Youth League must be the brains-trust and power-station of the spirit of African nationalism.'
– From the Manifesto of the Congress Youth League

Although Nelson had been elected to the Executive Committee of the Youth League, he was still just a beginner politician. He had some strong beliefs, but he didn't have much practical political experience. There were other responsibilities pulling at him: he was working full-time at Lazar Sidelsky's law office; he was studying part-time at the university; and he was now a married man. He also boxed whenever he could, to get exercise. Life was very full.

Several things happened in the next few years which influenced Nelson's political development. One of them was the 1946 strike by 70 000 members of the African Mine Workers' Union (AMWU) for better pay and working conditions. Although the strike was eventually lost, Nelson came to know JB Marks, the President of the AMWU and a member of the Communist Party, very well. He was impressed by the union's strong organisation, and had many discussions with Marks about the role of communism in South Africa.

Also in 1946, the government passed the Asiatic Land Tenure Act, which restricted the rights of Indians to live and work where they chose, and limited their right to buy property. To fight this, the Indian community launched a passive resistance* campaign, which lasted for two years. Although the government beat down this rebellion, it showed Nelson and others in the Youth League and the ANC how dedicated the Indian people could be in a political struggle.

At the beginning of 1947, Nelson completed the required three years of articles with the law firm. Now all he needed was a law degree and he would be a lawyer. He decided to go to law school full-time so that he could qualify more quickly. This was hard to do, because it meant they had to live on Evelyn's salary of £17 a month, but he and Evelyn agreed to try anyway.

Later that year, Nelson was elected to his first position in the ANC itself – he became an Executive Committee member of the Transvaal ANC. This marked a serious commitment to the organisation and the beginning of a life given almost entirely to the liberation movement. From that time onwards, Nelson Mandela spent more and more time on political work, and less and less on other commitments, including the law and his family.

Defying apartheid

6

In 1948, DF Malan's National Party was elected by white voters to form the national government of South Africa, and introduced 'apartheid' to the country. This Afrikaans word literally means 'separateness'. The National Party said that it meant 'separate development' – black and white people developing separately, each in their own areas and in the way that was best for them. In reality, however, it was a policy of white supremacy* and white domination.

In the decades to come, apartheid caused much suffering and misery. People were classified according to the colour of their skin. Laws enacted in the name of apartheid prevented people of different colours from living in the same neighbourhoods, going to the same schools, or doing the same work. Black people were not allowed to marry white people. They could not use the same parks, lifts or doors into public buildings. Black people could not vote. Those black children who managed to go to school got an education inferior to that of white children. Black people virtually became slaves in the land of their forefathers. Things became so bad that apartheid was eventually declared a 'crime against humanity' by the United Nations.

In 1948, however, this was all still to come. While the votes were being counted after the election, Mandela was at an ANC meeting. The question of how to deal with a Nationalist government was not discussed, because nobody believed that the Nats (as members of the National Party were often called) would win the election. The meeting lasted a long time, and when Mandela and Oliver Tambo left the building it was almost dawn. They saw trucks delivering the early edition of the newspapers. The headlines of the *Rand Daily Mail* shouted – 'NATS WIN!'

'This is terrible!' exclaimed a shocked Mandela. 'The Nats' insane policies will make our fight even more difficult.'

'That may be true,' said Tambo, 'but in a way this is a good thing. I like this.'

'How can you say that?' asked Mandela, surprised.

Tambo replied, 'Well, the very wickedness of their policies will help us. It will become clear to everyone exactly who our enemy is. People will unite in the struggle against them.'

Tambo's words were prophetic*, but the unity he predicted did not happen immediately. In January 1949, there were violent clashes in Durban between Africans and Indians. Many on both sides were killed. Leaders of the ANC and the Natal Indian Congress (NIC) joined to calm the people and restore order. This was an important experience for Mandela, who at the time was opposed to unity with the South African Indian Congress (SAIC). This incident made him see that people of different races could work together to solve a common problem.

Also in 1949, Mandela was elected to the National Executive of the ANC. He and other members of the Youth League brought a new focus to the ANC. Their Programme of Action called for civil disobedience to achieve their goals – in other words, protesting by disobeying the racist laws of the country.

In 1949 and 1950, the Nationalist government passed a number of Acts of Parliament which put its apartheid policy into effect. A number of people, including some leaders of the Communist Party who were also members of the ANC, were banned* by the government because they protested against these new laws. The ANC supported a call for a strike on 1 May 1950 to protest these bans. During the May Day demonstrations, 18 people were killed by the police.

The ANC and other groups with similar objectives – the South African Indian Congress, the African People's Organisation (a coloured group), the Communist Party of South Africa, and the Youth League – decided to call a one-day strike to protest the police killings on May Day, and to condemn the Suppression of Communism Act and the Group Areas Act, which had recently been passed by the government. The day of the strike was fixed for 26 June 1950, which was the day that the Suppression of Communism Act was to become law. This was the first time that such different groups had worked together for an event like this.

As he became more deeply involved in the freedom struggle, Mandela found himself working more and more closely with communists of all races. As his respect for them grew, his anti-communist prejudices evaporated.

Near the end of 1950, Mandela was elected as National President of the Youth League. He and others in the Youth League and on the ANC Executive began to think about what should be done next. It was decided to accept an idea suggested by Walter Sisulu – that there should be widespread, non-violent defiance of the government's unjust laws by volunteers. Mandela was appointed as Volunteer-in-Chief to co-ordinate the campaign nationally. It was the first time that he had been given such a big responsibility.

The organising of the campaign and the training of volunteers took months of hard work, but finally everything was ready. On 6 April 1952, demonstrations were held in some of the main cities of South Africa – Johannesburg, Pretoria, Port Elizabeth, Durban and Cape Town. April 6 was chosen because it was the three-hundred-year anniversary of the landing of Jan van Riebeeck at the Cape, an important day of celebration for the country's white people. Mandela spoke to a well-attended meeting of the Garment Workers' Union in Johannesburg, telling them about the Defiance Campaign that would soon begin. Then, on 26 June 1952, 250 African and Indian volunteers used 'Whites Only' entrances to railway stations, sat on 'Whites Only' park benches, deliberately left their passes at home, and stayed in the city after the curfew.

The police arrested thousands during the campaign, including Mandela. Although he was not scheduled to participate actively in the campaign until a while later, Mandela was actually arrested on the very first night of the Defiance Campaign. The police were out in force that night, roaming the streets, looking for anyone who looked as if they might be breaking the law. One policeman came across Mandela and some others at midnight just as they were leaving a meeting. Since the curfew for Africans was eleven o'clock at night, they were arrested. They were taken to Marshall Square police station together with a group of men who had been breaking the curfew on purpose.

During the six months of the campaign, more than 8 000 volunteers defied in all parts of the country. School teachers, dock workers, students, shopkeepers, ministers, farm workers, doctors, bus drivers – all sorts of people took part. They sang, 'Hey Malan! Open the jail doors. We want to come in!' Mandela travelled all over the country, meeting organising committees and talking to groups of volunteers, sorting out problems and encouraging his comrades.

The apartheid government was quite surprised at the size of the Campaign, and became more and more worried about the strength of the protest. Legislation was soon passed which gave the police greater powers: defiers could now be kept in jail without being brought to trial. Harsh penalties for civil disobedience were also introduced, including fines, imprisonment and hanging.

By the end of November 1952, Mandela and several other leaders were arrested and tried. They were found guilty of 'statutory communism'* and sentenced to nine months' imprisonment suspended for two years. The judge decided on this suspension because he believed that the ANC had tried to avoid violence throughout the Campaign.

Meanwhile, Mandela passed the necessary exams for a Law Certificate, which allowed him to practise as a lawyer. In August 1952, the law offices of Mandela and Tambo opened for business in central Johannesburg. At that time, it was the only black law practice in the country, and both men were kept very busy.

Mandela was soon elected President of the Transvaal ANC, and in December 1952 he became Deputy President of the ANC nationally. Mandela was banned soon after this, and confined to Johannesburg. It was the first of many banning orders*. Being banned meant that he was not allowed to participate in political or social gatherings. He couldn't even go to his own son's birthday party! In spite of these restrictions,

Mandela opening his law practice

Mandela continued to work quietly for the ANC and even taught some political classes to ANC members at this time.

At the end of 1952, the Defiance Campaign came to an end. During the Campaign, the membership of the ANC had risen from 7 000 to 100 000. The reputation of the organisation had grown, both inside and outside the country. While no laws had been repealed*, people had seen what could be accomplished when they worked together. For Mandela the Campaign had been his first taste of leadership on the grand scale – and he liked it.

7

'Dangerous. Do not feed.'

Although the Defiance Campaign had boosted the morale of the people, it made no difference to the Nationalist government's determination to implement its new apartheid policies. It continued to introduce new laws that took away the rights of black South Africans.

In August 1953, ZK Matthews, President of the ANC in the Cape Province, suggested that a national convention be called to discuss the problems facing the nation. 'This Convention could draw up a Freedom Charter for the democratic South Africa of the future,' he said. The Freedom Charter would be a document that reflected the hopes and wishes of people who were denied their human rights.

A National Action Council was formed to organise the Congress of the People. The ANC invited representatives from other organisations to take part – the Indian Congress, the Congress of Democrats (COD), and the Coloured People's Organisation (CPO). The last two had been formed recently by progressive white people and coloured people. The Council sent out leaflets asking, 'If you could make the laws, what would you do? ... Let the voices of all the people be heard!' The response was enormous. Thousands of suggestions about all kinds of issues were received from domestic workers, teachers, miners, factory workers, housewives, peasants, students, the unemployed ...

These suggestions were sent to the National Action Council where a draft Charter was written. The draft was circulated to branches of the organisations represented on the National

Action Council for discussion. Many of them made additional suggestions. Finally, Mandela and several others on the ANC's National Executive Committee approved the revised draft. Then 3 000 delegates were chosen from all over the country to come to a meeting to ratify* the document.

The Congress of the People took place on the chilly weekend of 25 and 26 June in 1955. People met at the football ground in Kliptown, a coloured township about 25 km south-west of Johannesburg. Not everyone could be there, however. Many of the leaders were banned, including Albert Luthuli, Walter Sisulu and Nelson Mandela. Some came in secret – Mandela and Sisulu drove to Kliptown together – and watched from the edge of the crowd as the clauses of the draft were read out, one by one, and the Freedom Charter was adopted. It promised the right to vote, to a home, to an education, and enough food to eat. It promised equality, a fair return for work done, and an end to discrimination. It was a document which promised a better future.

Members of the government felt threatened by the Congress of the People. They were convinced that the Freedom Charter was a treasonable document, designed to encourage people to overthrow the government, and they were determined to stop the Congress Alliance. In the years during and after the Defiance Campaign, the police carried out more than 1 000 raids of houses and offices of those fighting for democracy. During each raid they confiscated whatever documents, books and photographs they could find. They followed many democrats, watching them day and night sometimes; they tapped phone calls, and opened private letters before they were delivered. They were busy collecting information that could be used against members of the Congress Alliance. When they were ready, they took drastic action.

During the night of 5 December 1956, the police pounded on Mandela's door. He got out of bed, quickly got dressed and opened the door. 'What do you want?' he asked the three men standing there.

'We have a search warrant here, Mandela,' the policeman in charge said. Then he and two other policemen pushed their way in and searched the house. The noise woke up the children. They were afraid, but their father said to them, 'Be calm. Don't worry.'

Finally, the senior policeman took another paper out of his pocket and said, 'Mandela, we have a warrant for your arrest. Come with me.' Evelyn and the children looked on as he was taken away to the Johannesburg Central Prison, known as the Fort. Over the next few days it became clear that the police had swooped on many others that night – 156 of them altogether. Leaders of the liberation movement from all over the country and from all race groups were brought to Johannesburg, all arrested on charges of treason*.

Although conditions at the Fort were terrible – crowded cells, bad food, filthy sleeping mats and blankets – in a way it was an opportunity for Mandela and the others who had been arrested. Often, their banning orders had made it difficult for them to get together to talk about their common problems and campaigns. Now – and for the rest of the long trial that was to come – the leaders spent hours together. They realised that colour and race were not important because they had a common purpose.

During the trial, Mandela and the others were taken to court inside windowless police vans. They couldn't see anything outside, but they could hear. The road from the jail to the courthouse was lined with thousands of people who sang and chanted their support.

When they arrived at the court at the beginning of the trial, the accused and their lawyers were surprised to see that a huge cage had been erected inside the courtroom! The accused were supposed to sit locked inside it. As a joke, one of them put up a sign that said, 'Dangerous. Please do not feed.' Their lawyers protested, saying, 'We cannot permit this. Our clients cannot be treated like animals.' The magistrate agreed with them, and ordered that the cage be removed.

It took two whole days for the prosecutor* to read out the details of the charges against the accused. He said that they were members of a conspiracy to overthrow the government, and that they wanted to have a communist government instead. They planned to use violence to do this, he said. The Defiance Campaign and the Freedom Charter were part of this conspiracy, the prosecutor said in his charges. He accused the men and women of high treason, and called for the death penalty. This was only the beginning, though, of a long and grinding court battle that was to take more than four years.

Finally, the accused were granted bail. When Mandela arrived at his home in Orlando he found the house empty. His wife, Evelyn, had gone to her brother's house, taking the children and most of their possessions with her. Although Mandela was surprised at this sudden departure, the break-up of the marriage was not totally unexpected. For several years, Nelson and Evelyn had been developing in opposite directions. Evelyn had always thought in her heart that her husband's political activities were due to hot young blood. She believed that he would eventually settle down to his legal practice, preferably back in the Transkei, and that they would have a normal life. Over the years, too, she became increasingly religious. After the safe birth of her second daughter she joined the Jehovah's Witnesses, and tried to convince Nelson and her children of the rightness of this religion. For Mandela, on the other hand, the focus of his life was more and more the political battles he was helping to wage. He had long ago realised that he could not return to a simple life in the Transkei, nor could he share Evelyn's religious beliefs. They grew further and further apart. Their attitudes on many issues were totally opposite. Finally, Evelyn could not take the strain any more and decided to leave. They were divorced in 1957.

The trial resumed in January 1957. For the first six weeks, all the documents that the police had confiscated during their raids were entered into evidence. There were 12 000 of them, and each one had to be identified and accepted by the court. Hour after hour the prosecutor read document after document. His voice droned on and on in the hot courtroom. Even though the trialists were accused of a very serious crime, it was hard to pay attention to this monotonous process. Some of the accused dozed, some read, some did crossword puzzles, some played games – chess and Scrabble were popular. Mandela took the opportunity to catch up on work for his own legal practice, and often brought paperwork along so that he could prepare for some of the cases that were waiting for his attention.

This preliminary phase took nine months. At the end of that time, the state withdrew the charges against 64 people, including Albert Luthuli and Oliver Tambo. The magistrate decided that there was enough evidence for the rest of the accused to face charges of high treason in the Transvaal Supreme Court. The formal part of the trial began in Pretoria on 3 August 1958 and continued until 29 March 1961. During the trial a number of things happened, both inside and outside the court-room, that affected Nelson Mandela personally as well as the struggle to which he was very committed.

In 1957, Mandela had met a young social worker named Nomzamo Winifred Madikizela. Winnie, as she was known, was beautiful and lively, and Mandela was captivated. They were married less than a year later, in June 1958. Although she was not a political person when she met her husband-to-be, she

Nelson and Winnie on their wedding day

quickly learned how committed he was to the struggle for democracy. Years later, during an interview, she said, 'I knew when I married him that I married the struggle.' Before the end of the trial, they had two daughters – Zenani and Zindziswa.

In November 1958, another 61 of the accused were released. Only 30 were left to answer the charges in a new indictment* – that the accused had intended to act violently, and that violence was the policy of the ANC and its allies. Nelson Mandela was among the 30 people still on trial.

The trial seriously affected the law practice of Mandela and Tambo. They had to spend so much time in court that they didn't have the time to attend properly to their clients. The practice began falling apart, and eventually had to be closed. Mandela continued to do freelance* legal work throughout the trial, so there was some income, but Winnie's salary paid most of the bills.

In April 1959, a group headed by Robert Sobukwe – a former Youth League member – split away from the ANC in order to form the Pan Africanist Congress (PAC). White and Indian people and communists, they believed, had no useful part to play in the struggle for democracy. The ANC, they said, had weakened itself by allowing these groups to influence its members. The PAC was opposed to the Freedom Charter and the Congress Alliance, as well as to all forms of interracial co-operation.

The PAC announced that they would hold an anti-pass demonstration on 21 March. In Sharpeville, a township about 55 km south of Johannesburg, several thousand people marched to the police station. They were calm and unarmed. There were only 75 policemen, and they were nervous about the large number of people outside the fence surrounding the police station. They called in reinforcements. Then, although no order had been given to shoot, the police suddenly started to fire into the crowd, most of whom desperately tried to run away. When it was all over, 69 people lay dead and over 400 were injured. Many had been shot in the back as they fled.

The country and the world were shocked. Mandela and a few other ANC leaders – Walter Sisulu, Duma Nokwe and Joe Slovo – met in Johannesburg to decide what to do. They came up with a plan, which they discussed with Chief Luthuli, the President of the ANC; he agreed. On 26 March, Chief Luthuli burned his pass in Pretoria. He called on others to do the same, and announced a stay-at-home for 28 March, which he said should be a national day of mourning for the people who died at Sharpeville.

Mandela burning his pass book in the late 1950's

After Chief Luthuli had made his speech, the next part of the plan went into effect. Mandela and Duma Nokwe burned their passes in front of a large crowd in Orlando. Two days later, hundreds of thousands of people throughout the country responded to the ANC's call for a stay-at-home.

The government's answer was to declare a State of Emergency on 30 March 1960. This meant that the police could arrest people without a warrant and jail them for indefinite periods. Hundreds of men and women were arrested, including Mandela. Half a dozen policemen came to his house just after midnight. This time they were not so polite, and their search was more aggressive. They emptied drawers and cupboards, looked behind wardrobes, pulled books off shelves, and turned over mattresses in their search for anything incriminating*. The police took with them every piece of paper they could find, even family photos and the folk tales Mandela's mother had been dictating to him. This time it was Winnie who saw her husband handcuffed and taken away into the night. A week later the ANC and PAC were declared illegal organisations. The Treason Trialists remained in jail for the whole five months that the State of Emergency stayed in effect.

The trial finally drew to an end. When the court announced its verdict on 29 March 1961, hundreds were waiting. A court official had to shout, 'Order in the court!' several times before the judge could be heard. Judge Rumpff said that although the ANC wanted a 'radically and fundamentally different form of state', it did not have a policy of violence. He ended by saying, 'The accused are accordingly found not guilty and are discharged.'

Mandela and the other accused and their lawyers stood and hugged each other. The spectators cheered wildly. The crowd outside shouted and chanted slogans. Photographers took dozens of pictures. Everyone sang *Nkosi Sikelel' iAfrika*. It was a great victory for the African National

Congress – none of the 156 men and women accused of treason had been found guilty of the charge.

After all the excitement, Mandela didn't go home, but instead quietly disappeared. The harsher attitude of the government and the banning of the ANC meant that he and his comrades could no longer work in the same way that they had in the past. The ANC's National Working Committee decided that they had to work clandestinely* in the future. Mandela was chosen to go underground – to remain hidden from the police and to work secretly. He understood the need for this kind of decision, but it saddened him. He loved his family, and he knew that a life outside the law would separate him from that family.

It was the beginning of another phase of Mandela's life – an exciting but dangerous one.

The Treason Trialists

The Black Pimpernel

8

In 1960, the government had held a referendum* in which only the white people of the country were allowed to vote. They had decided that they wanted South Africa to be a republic, and did not want to recognise the British queen as South Africa's head of state any more. The ANC decided to hold a stay-at-home at the same time as the celebrations for Republic Day – 29, 30 and 31 March 1961. Because it was now illegal to organise strikes and stay-aways, it was decided that Mandela, who was working underground, would be the main organiser. Of course, he had a lot of help from his comrades in the Congress Alliance, but in this way they were a bit safer from arrest. The police quickly issued a warrant for Mandela's arrest, and he became the country's Number One Wanted Person.

Although he was in hiding, Mandela travelled all over the country to speak at meetings about the stay-at-home. He made sure that newspaper reporters knew what he was doing, phoning them with information, and sometimes even arranging secret meetings with them so that they could interview him. It was a risky business; there was always the danger that a reporter could turn him over to the police. It was necessary, though, to get the publicity that these radio and newspaper interviews provided. It was important for the people of the country to know what was happening.

Despite police harassment, the stay-at-home went ahead and thousands of people stayed away from their jobs. On 26 June 1961, a letter from Mandela to the people of the country was published in the newspapers. He thanked them for their participation in the stay-at-home and said, 'I shall fight the government side by side with you, inch by inch, and mile by mile, until victory is won ... Only through hardship, sacrifice and militant action can freedom be won. The struggle is my life. I will continue fighting for freedom until the end of my days.'

During an interview with a group of reporters about that time, Mandela said that maybe it was time to look at the way in which the Congress Alliance was trying to bring about change in the country. 'Non-violent passive resistance,' he said, 'is effective as long as your opposition adheres to the same rules as you do ... But if peaceful protest is met with violence, its efficacy* is at an end.' He was already thinking about forms of protest other than demonstrations and passive resistance.

> The time comes in the life of any nation when there remain only two choices: submit or fight. That time has now come to South Africa.
> – From the leaflet announcing the birth of Umkhonto we Sizwe

Although many in the Congress Alliance did not agree with them at this time, Mandela and Sisulu eventually managed to convince Chief Luthuli and the National Executive that it was necessary to change tactics. The decision that was finally taken was that the ANC itself would continue with its non-violent methods, but that a new organisation would be started to pursue a new form of struggle. This new organisation would be called Umkhonto we Sizwe, the Spear of the Nation, and its tool would be sabotage. It would aim to destroy things belonging to the state – electricity pylons, railway lines, unoccupied post offices, and so on – but would not target people. Mandela was put in charge of establishing this new army of the people.

In order not to be discovered by the police and the Special Branch*, Mandela often wore disguises. Sometimes he was a poor labourer or a gardener, wearing the overalls that most workers wore. Sometimes he pretended to be a chauffeur, wearing a long coat and peaked hat. He let his hair grow longer, and grew a beard. Sometimes he wore glasses. A name he often used was David Motsamayi. Whatever his disguise, he continued to travel around the country, making his preparations for Umkhonto we Sizwe.

While he was underground, he stayed in many different places. Because he popped up unexpectedly here and there around the country, the newspapers nicknamed Mandela 'the Black Pimpernel'. This name came from a story-book character called the Scarlet Pimpernel, who lived at the time of the French Revolution. He was very good at escaping from the soldiers who were trying to arrest and kill him. Mandela's daring and courage were admired by many people.

While he was in hiding, Mandela spent a lot of his time reading and studying. He didn't know much about armies or how they worked, so while he was staying at the flat of Wolfie Kodesh, a member of the Congress of Democrats, he asked for some advice. Kodesh, who had been a soldier in World War 2, recommended some books on weapons and guerilla war. Mandela asked a variety of people to help him establish the new army, and also to make weapons for it. For instance, he recruited Jack Hodgson, who like Kodesh had fought in World War 2 and knew quite a bit about bombs; Wolfie Kodesh also helped with this. Hodgson experimented with different chemicals and other materials in his Johannesburg flat. His wife, Rica, often complained that he kept burning holes in the carpets with his experiments, but she too was committed to the struggle so she didn't really mind.

When some sample home-made bombs and hand grenades were ready to be tried out, Kodesh took Mandela, Hodgson and a few others to a brick factory nearby. It was late at night so the place was dark and deserted. The men took a bomb out of the boot of the car and carried it over to a big hole in the ground where sand had been dug up to make bricks. Hodgson climbed into the hole, set the timer on the bomb, and quickly climbed out again. They all stood back and waited. Five minutes, ten minutes, fifteen minutes. Nothing happened. Should they go into the hole to check the bomb? What if it exploded the minute they got near?

Finally, Hodgson and Kodesh decided to go in. They made a few adjustments to the bomb, and then climbed out of the hole. Almost immediately there was a huge and very loud explosion! Dust and rocks flew high into the air! Quickly the men ran back to the car. As they were speeding away, Mandela exclaimed excitedly, 'Now we can do it! Now I know we can do it!'

The date for the first action of the armed struggle was set for the night of 16 December 1961 – the Day of the Covenant, when white people celebrated their victory over the Zulu king Dingane at Blood River. The day was symbolic of white supremacy over black people and so it was a good choice for the beginning of a campaign against that supremacy. Bombs were set off that night in Johannesburg, Port Elizabeth and Durban, destroying government offices, electricity lines, railway lines, telephone networks and post offices. Leaflets were distributed all over the country, announcing the formation of Umkhonto we Sizwe and what it stood for. The armed struggle had begun. The police now wanted to catch Mandela more than ever. Life on the run was getting more and more dangerous for him.

The next month, in January 1962, Mandela was smuggled across the border into Botswana. He went on to Accra in Ghana, where he met his old friend, Oliver Tambo, who had been sent out of the country to organise support for the ANC. Together they visited several countries in Africa – Tanzania, Algeria, Egypt, Tunisia, Ethiopia, Morocco, Mali,

Guinea, Sierra Leone, Liberia and Senegal – as well as England, in order to raise money and other support for the movement. Mandela then went back to Ethiopia to get some military training. He had lessons in physical combat, weapons training, making and using bombs, military history and strategy, and how to command an army. Then, less than six months after he had left, he returned to South Africa.

Shortly after his return, Mandela went to Natal to tell Chief Luthuli about his experiences abroad. On his way back to Johannesburg on 5 August 1962 he was arrested just outside the little Natal town of Howick. It was the end of the activities of the Black Pimpernel. Mandela was taken to Pretoria and put on trial for inciting workers to strike (during the May stay-at-home) and for leaving the country without a passport.

A little while earlier, Mandela had begun studying by correspondence for his LL B (law) degree. While he was in jail waiting for his trial to begin, he wanted to continue studying. He asked his jailers for a book called *The Law of Torts*, which is about a certain branch of the law. When he heard about this, the head of the prison came to his cell and said, 'Mandela, why do you want a book about torches? Are you planning more sabotage?' Mandela tried to keep a straight face as he explained to the man that he didn't really want a *toort* – the Afrikaans word for torch.

When the trial finally started, Mandela came to court wearing a traditional Xhosa leopard-skin kaross. With his 1,8 m height and his royal air, Mandela made an imposing figure. The people in the court were amazed; they were more used to suits and ties in courtrooms. 'I chose traditional dress,' Mandela later wrote in his autobiography, *Long Walk to Freedom,* 'to emphasise ... that I was a black African walking into a white man's court.'

Mandela was found guilty and sentenced to five years in prison.

9

Prepared to die

Mandela spent the first three months of his sentence at Pretoria Local Prison. The huge red-brick complex of buildings was already well-known to Mandela from the days of the Treason Trial. There he became familiar with the inhumane way in which African prisoners were treated in South African jails.

After he had been convicted, Mandela's own clothes were taken away from him and he was given standard prison clothing – short trousers, khaki shirt, thin canvas jacket, sandals, and a cloth cap. He refused to wear the shorts because he felt that he was being treated like a 'boy' by his captors. He also objected strongly to the poor quality food that the African prisoners were expected to eat. The commander of the prison agreed that he could wear long trousers and that he could eat whatever he wanted to, but only if he agreed to spend his time in isolation. In his pride, Mandela decided to agree.

It was a terrible experience, he discovered, to be in solitary confinement, cut off from all contact with his fellow prisoners, in his cell with nothing to do for 23 hours out of every 24 except watch the cockroaches and count the bricks in the walls. Twice a day he was let out of the cell for half an hour, into an empty courtyard, for a bit of exercise. In the cell, a bare light bulb burned constantly above his head; sometimes Mandela didn't know whether it was day or night. After a few weeks of this, he swallowed his pride and asked to be returned to the general prison population. Wearing shorts and eating cold unsweetened porridge were, he felt, a small price to pay to avoid solitary.

After three months, Mandela was transferred to Robben Island. On this occasion, he would stay only a few weeks.

Life on *Die Eiland*, as the Afrikaans-speaking warders referred to it, was not much different from life in Pretoria Local. The warders, though, were a rough lot. When Mandela first arrived at Robben Island, he was greeted by warders shouting, '*Dit is die Eiland! Hier gaan julle vrek!*' (This is the Island. Here you will die!) Much to their surprise, the warders found that they were unable to intimidate* Mandela and some of the other political prisoners.

'Prison not only robs you of your freedom, it attempts to take away your identity. Everyone wears a uniform, eats the same food, follows the same schedule. It is by definition a purely authoritarian state that tolerates no independence or individuality. As a freedom fighter and as a man, one must fight against the prison's attempt to rob one of these qualities.'

– From *Long Walk to Freedom*, page 321

Suddenly one morning, Mandela was told to pack up his few belongings. He was taken back to Pretoria, although he had no idea why. A few days later, he was called to one of the prison offices. He was shocked to see Rusty Bernstein, Denis Goldberg, Bob Hepple, James Kantor, Ahmed Kathrada, Govan Mbeki, Raymond Mhlaba, Andrew Mlangeni, Elias Motsoaledi and Walter Sisulu. Among these men were the top leadership – the High Command – of Umkhonto we Sizwe. 'Something has gone very wrong,' he said to himself.

Something had indeed gone very wrong. The police had been watching Liliesleaf Farm in Rivonia for some time, because they suspected it was Umkhonto's headquarters. Finally in July 1963 they swooped. They arrested all the people they found there, and also took away dozens of documents, many of them dealing with the armed struggle, as well as books about the tactics of war and popular uprisings in other countries.

Luckily, two members of the High Command, Joe Slovo and Bram Fischer, had not been there that day.

The Rivonia Trial, as it came to be known, began in October 1963 and lasted for eleven months. While Percy Yutar, the prosecutor, was presenting his case, Mandela continued studying for his law degree. He was doing correspondence studies through the University of London. Perhaps concentrating on these studies helped him forget for a while about the difficult situation in which he found himself. In any event, he wrote several exams during that trial – and passed them all!

The prosecution was determined to show that the ANC and Umkhonto we Sizwe were using violence to try to overthrow the government, that they were working together with communists to reach this goal, and that they were engaged in guerilla warfare. When Mandela was asked how he pleaded, he said, 'It is not I, but the government that should be in the dock. I plead not guilty.' All the other accused pleaded not guilty as well.

When the time came for the defence to make its case, it was decided that Mandela would make a statement from the dock. This was an opportunity to tell the nation and the world what the struggle of the ANC and Umkhonto we Sizwe was all about.

Mandela spoke for four hours. He outlined the history of the liberation movement and the non-violent way in which it had tried to bring about change for nearly 50 years. He explained the reasons why the decision had been taken to begin a campaign of sabotage. He talked at length about the life faced by the black people of South Africa, and why they believed it was necessary to fight for a better life. He ended his statement with words which were to become known throughout the world:

'During my lifetime I have dedicated myself to this struggle of the African people. I have fought against white domination, and I have fought against black domination. I have cherished the ideal of a democratic and free society in which all persons live together in harmony and with equal opportunities. It is an ideal which I hope to live for and to achieve. But if needs be, it is an ideal for which I am prepared to die.'

And the world was listening. The publicity surrounding the trial had made the world sit up and take notice. All-night vigils were held in St Paul's Cathedral in London. Protests were made by international trade unions. The United Nations Security Council called for the unconditional release of the Rivonia Trialists and all other political prisoners. The apartheid government ignored it all.

Bob Hepple agreed to turn state witness and was released; he then fled the country to avoid giving evidence against the other accused. At the end of the Prosecution's case, the judge discharged James Kantor because there was not enough evidence against him. On 11 June 1964, the verdicts for the others were read out to a very tense courtroom. The families of the accused were watching from the spectators' gallery, anxiously waiting to hear the fate of their loved ones. Rusty Bernstein was found not guilty and released. Ahmed Kathrada was found guilty on one charge and not guilty on the others. The rest of the accused were all found guilty as charged. They spent a nervous night waiting to be sentenced. The next day the judge spoke to a packed courtroom. 'The sentence in the case of all the accused,' he said in a quiet voice, 'will be life imprisonment.'

All the accused and their families watching from the gallery breathed a sigh of relief. They had been expecting the death penalty, and life imprisonment seemed almost like a reprieve*.

10 Prisoner number 466/64

The night after they had been sentenced to life imprisonment, the group was transferred to Robben Island. This time, Mandela became Prisoner number 466/64 – the 466th prisoner to arrive in 1964. He was 46 years old when he arrived on the island for the second time.

Mandela and his friends found that a new maximum security section had been built for political prisoners. It consisted of cells built around three sides of a courtyard; the fourth side was a high grey stone wall. The cells were like small boxes, three metres by two. When Mandela stretched out on his sleeping mat, his head and toes could touch the cell walls. The cell had one small barred window facing the courtyard. There were two doors. One was a metal grille, which was kept closed whenever the prisoner was in the cell. The other was a strong wooden door which was closed over the grille door at night. There was a mat to sleep on and a metal bucket known as a bally, which was used as a toilet. This was all that the cell contained. This small, barren place would be Nelson Mandela's home for the next 18 years.

The routine in the early months was basic and hardly ever changed. The prisoners were woken up at half past five in the morning by the clanging of a brass bell. They had to clean their cells and ballies before breakfast. That meal consisted of mielie meal porridge and some 'coffee' made from ground roasted mielies instead of coffee beans. Then came inspection. After that, the group went out to the courtyard where they were each given a hammer and led to a pile of rocks about the size of soccer balls. They had to break the rocks down into gravel. They worked until lunch, when they ate boiled mielies. Stone-breaking continued until four o' clock in the afternoon. Then they had half an hour to clean themselves up – they washed in cold sea water which was piped to the courtyard. A supper of mielie pap and vegetables, with small portions of gristly meat every second day, was eaten at half past four in the afternoon. Then the prisoners were free to move around the courtyard until eight o' clock in the evening when they were locked into their cells.

Prisoners working in the prison yard on Robben Island

The routine was different on weekends. The prisoners were locked into their cells for the entire day, except for half an hour of exercise each day.

The lights were never turned out, and a warder patrolled for the whole night. After lock-up no reading, writing or talking was allowed. If the warder caught the prisoners doing any of these things, they could be punished. One of the prisoners got the idea of putting a bit of sand on the floor of the corridor, so that they could hear the warder coming. After that, they could chat quietly among themselves until they heard the sound of his footsteps crunching over the sand.

After several months, the work of the prisoners was suddenly changed. One morning they were taken to another part of the island, where there was a lime quarry. For the next 13 years, Mandela and the others dug lime from between layers of hard rock. There were both good and bad sides to working in the quarry. On the bad side, the strong sun glared down on the white lime, making a very bright light. That light, together with the lime dust, damaged the eyesight of many of the prisoners. From that time onwards, Mandela had trouble with his eyes.

On the good side, working together in groups in the quarry gave the prisoners a chance to talk to each other. Also, they were sometimes expected to walk from the prison to the lime quarry, about a twenty minute walk. It was good, Mandela felt, to be able to walk and work outside of that depressing courtyard. He could feel the breeze, see birds flying overhead, watch a buck running in the distance. Sometimes he could almost believe he was free!

There were many restricting regulations in prison. For example, each of the political prisoners could receive only one letter and one visit every six months; those letters that were allowed through were usually censored*. Sometimes so much was crossed out with black ink or cut out with a razor blade that it was very hard to make sense of what had been written. The prison clothes had to be worn in a certain way; for example, the three buttons of the jacket always had to be buttoned during inspection. Warders had to be treated in a certain way by the prisoners – a prisoner could never sit down in the presence of a warder; he had to stand up and take off his cap. Radios and newspapers were not permitted. There were many other regulations. If any of them were not obeyed, the prisoner could be punished by being put in isolation or being denied meals.

Mandela was once punished for picking up and reading a newspaper that had been left on a chair by a warder. Like all the other political prisoners, he was starving for news of the outside world, and wanted to know what was happening to the ANC and to the struggle. He couldn't resist the temptation when he saw the paper lying there. When he was caught, he was sentenced to three days in solitary confinement and no meals. Instead of the usual prison food (which was poor enough), he was given only rice water to drink – water in which rice had been cooked.

Mandela and the others realised that their struggle for liberation was not over just because they had been put in prison. Inside the prison they fought for their rights as human beings. 'I was now on the sidelines ...' Mandela later wrote. 'I was in a different and smaller arena ... for whom the only audience was ourselves and our oppressors ... We would fight inside as we had fought outside.'

This decision was important because it gave them a way to survive within a system that was designed not only to hold them prisoner but to take away their dignity. It gave them a goal and that helped to make their imprisonment bearable.

The ANC prisoners quickly formed a committee which they called the High Organ. There were four people on it – Walter Sisulu, Govan Mbeki, Raymond Mhlaba and Nelson Mandela. All of them had been on the National Executive Committee of the ANC. Later, a fifth member was added to the High Organ on a rotating basis, so that different people were members at different times. It was not necessary for these rotating members to be ANC members; they belonged to political groups like the PAC, the Non-European Unity Movement, the Azanian Peoples' Organisation and others.

One of the most important things that the High Organ did was to co-ordinate protests against the bad prison conditions. Over the years, much was accomplished – an end to the hated short trousers, more frequent letters and visits from relatives, permission to study, better food, equal treatment of political prisoners from different race groups, permission to be in the courtyard on weekends, the provision of board games and playing cards. It took years for some of these changes to be made (newspapers were not allowed until 1980, for example), and privileges could be withdrawn by the authorities at any time. But the fact that people were working together helped to make the long struggle bearable.

Sometimes there was also help from the outside. The International Committee of the Red Cross sent representatives to the prison regularly. Over the years these representatives heard the prisoners' complaints and tried to put pressure on the government to change some of the worst regulations. Politicians such as Helen Suzman, a liberal member of parliament, also visited the prisoners occasionally, and heard their complaints and tried to convince the Minister of Justice to improve this or that problem.

Competitions were sometimes arranged by the High Organ to give the prisoners something fun and interesting to do. Mandela always took part in the draughts competition. In some years, he won the grand prize – a chocolate bar. In his autobiography, Mandela wrote, 'My style of play was slow and deliberate; my strategy was conservative. I carefully considered the ramifica-tions of every option and took a long time between moves ... It is my preferred mode of operating, not only in draughts but in politics.'

The High Organ encouraged political prisoners to study by correspondence, either for their matriculation certificates or for university degrees. Mandela was allowed to continue his studies with the University of London. Unfortunately, he didn't always have all the textbooks he needed because some of them were banned. Despite this, he managed to complete his LL B degree while he was on Robben Island.

In later years, many people in the liberation movement referred to Robben Island as 'The University'. This was not because so many of the prisoners registered for various academic courses. Rather, it was because the High Organ arranged for unofficial political courses to be held, especially for the younger prisoners who did not know very much about politics and the history of the struggle. Walter Sisulu taught the history of the ANC. This started as a few lectures, but eventually turned into a two-year programme of study. There were also courses on the 'History of the Indian Struggle', the 'History of the Coloured People in South Africa', political economy, and Marxism. Especially in the early years, these courses had to be held secretly because they were not allowed by prison regulations.

Different ways were worked out for communicating with the common-law prisoners in other parts of the prison, and also with people outside of the prison. Messages were passed to one another by writing them in milk; the writing was invisible until sprayed with the disinfectant that was given to the prisoners to clean their ballies. Sometimes a tiny piece of paper with a message written on it was put in a matchbox with a false bottom. Some messages were wrapped in plastic and left at the bottom of the food barrels that came from the prison's central kitchen; the messages were then passed out of the prison by sympathetic common-law prisoners and friendly warders.

In 1968, Mandela was visited by his mother, his son Makgatho, his daughter Makaziwe and his sister Mabel. It was wonderful to see them again, and he drank up their news like a thirsty man. Unfortunately, they were only allowed 45 minutes to talk and then the visit was over. A few weeks later, Mandela got a telegram informing him that his mother had died of a heart attack. Although he promised not to try to escape, he was refused permission to attend her funeral.

In July 1969, he got more bad news. His eldest son, Thembekile, had been killed in a car accident. Again, Mandela was refused permission to go to the funeral. He was devastated. It was one of the lowest points of his whole time in prison. Only the strict self-control that he had developed to cope with prison life and the sympathetic understanding of his friends helped him through this bad time.

> 'The challenge for every prisoner, particularly every political prisoner, is how to survive prison intact, how to emerge from prison undiminished ... Prison is designed to break one's spirit and destroy one's resolve.
> To do this, the authorities attempt to exploit every weakness, demolish every initiative, negate all signs of individuality – all with the idea of stamping out that spark that makes each of us human and each of us who we are.'
> – From *Long Walk to Freedom*, page 375–376

Aside from these particularly cruel incidents, one of the things that Mandela found the hardest to bear during his prison years was that he saw so little of his wife and children, and that he could not help them in their times of trouble. It was not always easy for Winnie to get permission to visit her husband. Mandela saw Zeni and Zindzi when they were toddlers, and then not again through their growing years. And he knew that his wife was being harassed by the authorities. She was arrested several times, and spent months in jail more than once. It was not an easy life for her, but she endured it with strength.

Outside the prison, the Nationalist government wanted very much to get other countries to recognise the bantustans or 'independent homelands' it was trying to set up. It was especially interested in getting formal recognition for the Transkei, because this was the first homeland granted 'independence' and the government was hoping to set an example. The Nationalist government had given the power there to Mandela's nephew, KD Matanzima. Mandela and many others were against this and continued to support the traditional king, Sabata. In 1976, Minister of Justice, Prisons and Police Jimmy Kruger came to Robben Island to see Mandela. 'If you agree to live in the Transkei and accept it as an independent homeland,' he said, 'you can be free tomorrow.' The government believed that if an important person like Nelson Mandela accepted what the government was doing in the Transkei, many other people in the country would support it.

'Your whole homelands policy is wrong,' retorted Mandela. 'I cannot accept this offer.'

Another development outside the prison was the growth of the Black Consciousness Movement, one of whose leaders was Steve Biko. The philosophy of this movement attracted especially the younger activists. They believed that it was necessary to find pride in themselves as black Africans, and that they had to find their own liberation without the help of people of any other colour. In some ways, this was similar to the way in which Mandela and the other Youth Leaguers had felt many years earlier. The young people now defied the authority of the white government and many were sent to prison. Even there, they were defiant, sometimes to an extent which surprised the older generation already there.

From the late 1970s onwards, and continuing into the 1980s, the activities of Umkhonto we Sizwe inside the country steadily increased. There were many bombings of power stations, police stations and other symbols of the apartheid government. Many of these brave freedom fighters were caught. Some of them were sent to Robben Island where they were able to tell the prisoners who were already there about what was happening in the country and about the liberation movement in exile. Mandela often spent many hours talking to these men.

The ANC members in exile had made many friends overseas. People in several countries had formed anti-apartheid movements and were trying to help the liberation struggle in whatever way they could. They called on their governments to cut all economic, sporting and cultural ties with South Africa. The slogan of one of the main campaigns was 'Free Nelson Mandela and All Political Prisoners'. The political prisoners on Robben Island, especially Mandela, were becoming famous throughout the world as symbols of resistance.

One day, in March 1982, the commanding officer of the prison unexpectedly told Mandela to pack his things. 'Get ready to move,' he said.

'Where am I going?' Mandela asked.

'I can't tell you,' the officer replied.

Mandela put his few personal possessions into some cardboard boxes. The same thing happened to three of the other Rivonia Trialists – Walter Sisulu, Raymond Mhlaba and Andrew Mlangeni. (Ahmed Kathrada was to follow a few months later.) A few hours later, they were taken by five armed warders onto a boat to Cape Town. The sea was very stormy, and Mandela wondered if his life would end by drowning. Finally, however, they reached the shore. Mandela and the others were put into the back of an enclosed truck and driven off into the night.

11   Closer to freedom

W hen the truck finally stopped, the four men found themselves within the walls of Pollsmoor Prison, a few kilometres from Cape Town. Pollsmoor Prison is situated near the beautiful Tokai Forest, beneath the mountains of the Cape Peninsula. The men from Robben Island were not allowed to mix with the other prisoners at all. They were kept by themselves, on the third floor of an isolated part of the prison. They shared a large, clean room which had an attached toilet and shower section. Their prison room had beds and sheets – a luxury they hadn't had for most of their time on Robben Island.

Attached to their communal cell was an open terrace where the men could sit or walk in the sun. Unfortunately, the terrace had very high walls, so they could not see any of the beautiful scenery for which the Cape is famous. All they could see was a bit of blue sky. Mandela asked for a number of steel drums, cut in half and filled with good soil. He kept a successful vegetable garden for several years, regularly supplying the warders and the prison's main kitchen with fresh onions, cabbages, beans, spinach, carrots, cucumbers, lettuce, tomatoes and other tasty vegetables. He even grew strawberries.

The prisoners never knew why they had been transferred from Robben Island to this place, but they guessed it might be because of their political influence on the younger prisoners that were arriving on the island.

Life at Pollsmoor was not that different – it was also a

prison, after all. Some things were worse, though – the dampness of the cell walls, the lack of privacy because they no longer had individual cells, and the loss of the wild scenery that they had enjoyed on the island. Worst of all was that they were isolated from the other prisoners.

Because of the newspapers and radio that they were allowed to have, Mandela and his comrades were able to keep up with what was happening in the world outside. They heard, for instance, that the struggle was escalating*. On the ANC's side, sabotage activity was becoming more and more frequent, and more government targets were being hit. The government was responding by becoming more and more repressive. It even carried out military raids on neighbouring countries, saying that the army was attacking ANC bases.

The year 1984 was an important one for Nelson Mandela. He began to be allowed contact visits by members of his family. This meant that they could be in the same room with him during visits instead of on the other side of a glass partition, speaking through a microphone. For the first time in 21 years he was able to hold his wife in his arms, to hug his children, to cuddle his grandchildren. It was wonderful!

In January 1985, President PW Botha announced in parliament that he was willing to release Mandela and other political prisoners, but that they would first have to reject violence as a method of struggle. Mandela consulted his fellow prisoners, and they decided that such an offer could not be accepted. Mandela prepared an answer, and sent it out of prison to be read out at a rally in Soweto on 10 February 1985. His daughter Zindzi read the message to a stadium packed with thousands of people of all races and ages. In it Mandela said that he could not reject violence while the government was still using it. At the same time, he said, he did not want violence; negotiation, not war, was the path that should be followed. He stressed his loyalty to the ANC and to the people. 'Only free men can negotiate,' he went on. 'I cannot and will not give any undertaking at a time when you and I, the people, are not free. Your freedom and mine cannot be separated. I will return.' When Zindzi finished reading the message, the stadium erupted! People cheered, whistled, toyi-toyied. Freedom was so close, they felt that day, that they could almost touch it!

Later that same year, Mandela was sent to Volks Hospital in Cape Town for surgery for an enlarged prostate gland. It was not a serious operation, but he had to stay in the hospital for a few days. While there, he was visited by Kobie Coetsee, the Minister of Justice. Mandela was amazed! A cabinet minister making a seemingly casual hospital visit to a prisoner! But there was a reason for it. Some time earlier Mandela had written to Coetsee asking to see him. Coetsee had never answered the letter, but this visit seemed to be his unofficial response. Campaigns to free Mandela and to isolate South Africa were growing internationally, as was opposition to the government inside the country. It was becoming more and more difficult for the government to ignore Mandela and the ANC. This was the first of many meetings between them.

When Mandela was finally brought back to Pollsmoor Prison, he was not returned to his third-floor cell with the other prisoners. Instead, he was given a place of his own in another part of the prison. The government recognised his importance, both as a leader of the ANC and as an international anti-apartheid symbol, and was trying to isolate him from the other political prisoners. He had one cell for sleeping, another to use as a study, and an area in which to exercise. The cells were damp, and eventually this caused lung problems for Mandela. He also missed his rooftop garden.

Mandela was very lonely with this new arrangement because he saw nobody except his jailers. However, he put his isolation to good use. He decided, after a lot of thought, to try to begin discussions with the government. He believed that if negotiations of some sort did not begin soon, they never would. There would be more and more violence on both sides and thousands of people would die. He did not want this to happen. However, he was not at all sure that Sisulu and the others would agree with him about the need for talks.

Better not to tell them, he thought. If my plan works, good. If it doesn't, they can always say that I was wrong, that I was speaking only for myself and not for the movement.

Meanwhile, things were moving faster outside the prison. The ANC had issued a call to the people of the country to 'make South Africa ungovernable'. The people responded willingly. South Africa was in turmoil. There were many demonstrations, strikes, school boycotts and attacks on people who were thought to be government spies. In May 1986 the South African Defence Force (SADF) bombed ANC communities in Botswana, Zambia and Zimbabwe. In June, President Botha declared a state of emergency in many parts of the country, giving more power to the police and army to fight the people. On and off, this would continue until 1990 with thousands of people being detained without trial and many being tortured by the police.

By sending letters to Kobie Coetsee, Mandela repeatedly asked for a meeting with President Botha. There was no response for a long time. However, at about this time Mandela began to be taken out of the prison every now and then for drives through the countryside and the city. Sometimes he and his warders, who did not wear uniforms on these outings, even had tea at some café or other. Mandela was never recognised. After all, the last picture anybody had seen of him had been taken in 1966!

Finally, in May 1988, Mandela began having meetings with a committee set up by the government. Kobie Coetsee was in charge of this committee. Also on it were General Willemse, the Commissioner of Prisons, Fanie van der Merwe, the Director General of Prisons, and Dr Niel Barnard, head of the National Intelligence Service. The talks went on for months.

Mandela found he had to start from the beginning, with the history of the ANC, because the men facing him did not know very much about it. He went on to outline the ANC's position on things like the armed struggle, its alliance with the Communist Party and majority rule. It was time, Mandela said, to seriously begin talks between the ANC and the government, and that the ANC headquarters in Lusaka should be contacted to arrange this.

His audience was very hard to convince.

Later in 1988, Mandela had a cough that got worse and worse. He was taken from Pollsmoor Prison to Tygerberg Hospital, where it was discovered that he had tuberculosis. After two months of treatment, Mandela was driven to the town of Paarl, about 55 km from Cape Town. There he was taken to a cottage in the grounds of Victor Verster Prison. The cottage had several bedrooms, a study for Mandela to work in, a kitchen, a sitting room, a swimming pool – and a very high fence with razor wire on top of it and guards at the gate. Although very comfortable, it was still a prison.

'This place,' said Kobie Coetsee, 'is halfway between confinement and freedom.' When Mandela heard this, he knew the time was coming closer when he would be free.

During 1989, Mandela continued his meetings with representatives of the government. He was also allowed more and more visits from other people. Members of his family came often to see him, and on his 71st birthday that year nearly everyone was there, including his grandchildren. It was a wonderful day for a man who had been deprived of his family for so long. Mandela was also visited by some of his comrades from Pollsmoor Prison, and by a number of delegations from the liberation movement and other groups inside the country. It seemed, sometimes, as if he was not in prison at all. Some said that he was a president-in-waiting, and believed that he would soon be the president of the country.

In July 1989, Mandela had a short meeting with President Botha. Mandela was nervous, but managed to hide it; years of concealing his emotions in prison had given him a lot of practice. The government men who accompanied Mandela seemed to be more nervous than he was, fussing about his clothes and how he had knotted his tie. One of them even knelt at his feet to tie his shoelaces properly.

Mandela and Botha had tea and chatted about small things. Only at the end of the half-hour visit did Mandela raise his concerns. He asked that he and other political prisoners be released from prison.

'I cannot do that, Mandela,' said Botha. And that was that. The meeting was over.

The next month, Botha resigned as state president. He had recently had a heart attack, and his health was not good. Also, he had less and less support from the members of his own party, who thought that he was no longer the right man to lead them. His place as head of the National Party and as President of South Africa was taken by FW de Klerk.

As soon as De Klerk took these positions, Mandela read everything he could about the man, and also things that he had written. He decided that De Klerk was a pragmatist, a practical man who would do what was necessary for South Africa. Mandela was right, and in October 1989, De Klerk released several political prisoners, including Walter Sisulu, Raymond Mhlaba, Ahmed Kathrada, Andrew Mlangeni, Elias Motsoaledi, Jeff Masemola, Wilton Mkwayi, and Oscar Mpetha. (Govan Mbeki had been released some time earlier, probably as a test to see how a political prisoner would behave when he was released.) De Klerk also began to remove some of the apartheid legislation that affected the different races in the country.

Mandela and De Klerk finally met on 1 December 1989. They found that they agreed about many things, although there were even more that they disagreed about. Mandela returned to his cottage prison feeling very optimistic.

Two months later, on 2 February 1990, during his speech at the opening of parliament, De Klerk made a stunning announcement – he was unbanning the ANC, the SACP and 32 other political organisations. Furthermore, he said, he would abolish capital punishment, and all political prisoners would be released soon. 'The time for negotiation has arrived,' he said.

Expectations were running high. When would Mandela be released? No negotiations could begin until he was free. The world was waiting. It didn't have to wait long.

On the afternoon of 11 February 1990, Nelson Mandela walked out through the gates of Victor Verster Prison, towards a crowd of thousands and saluted the cheering people. He was 71 years old, and had spent a total of 27 years in prison. But he was free at last!

Mandela and De Klerk

12

Negotiating for democracy

In some ways, the Mandela who came out of prison was a very different man from the one who went in. The sociable young lawyer and freedom fighter had become a very private, self-controlled person. He did not show his emotions easily or share them with other people. Mandela himself felt that the conditions he had undergone in prison for so long had matured him. He felt that the years in prison were not wasted years, but had given him and his comrades time to think and plan and learn. One of the lessons he had learned was the importance of reconciliation, of trying to find the best way to make peace between people who had very different beliefs about what the future should hold.

'In prison my anger towards whites decreased,' he wrote, 'but my hatred for the system grew.' Mandela was determined to replace the apartheid system that, despite some changes in recent years, still held the country in its grip. It was not going to be easy.

When he walked out of Victor Verster Prison, Mandela faced the first of many challenges. Instead of the dozen or so people he had expected, he saw a crowd of thousands. Hundreds of photographers took pictures as he walked towards them. Radio and television interviewers crowded around with their microphones, shouting to get his attention.

After a few minutes, he got into a car to be taken to Cape Town. All along the 55 km route, people were waiting for him. They waved and shouted their greetings as his car passed. Mandela was surprised that so many of them were white; that certainly would not have happened in the days before he went to prison. It seemed like a different country, he thought.

The car took Mandela to the Grand Parade, a large square in the city centre. There, from a balcony of the Cape Town City Hall, he addressed a rally of thousands of people. He reminded them – and the millions watching on television – that although he was now out of prison he was not truly free because apartheid was still alive. Despite this, he was hopeful that things would work out well. 'The sight of freedom looming on the horizon,' he said, 'should encourage us to redouble our efforts.'

This was the first of many meetings, rallies and demonstrations at which Mandela spoke. For the next six months, he spent more time travelling than at home. After spending a short time with his wife, Winnie, at her home in Johannesburg, he travelled to Lusaka to meet with the leadership of the ANC. Although the ANC had been unbanned, the leadership and many others remained outside South Africa. Mandela explained everything that he had said in his talks with the government. He knew that some of the members of the ANC's National Executive Committee (NEC) were worried that he was trying to act on his own, but he promised them that all he wanted was for the ANC and the South African government to talk together so that there could be an end to apartheid. He would do whatever the organisation wanted him to do from now on. The NEC members accepted what he said, and elected him deputy president of the ANC.

In this and other journeys, Mandela met with the leaders of countries in Africa, Asia, Europe and North America. Everywhere he went, he thanked all the groups and individuals who had helped the ANC during the years of struggle, in ways both large and small. He also told them that the struggle was not yet over, and asked them to continue helping for a while longer. Sanctions had to stay in place, he said.

Pressure should continue to be put on the government in Pretoria until it had made the changes that would truly free all the country's people.

During his first trip abroad, Mandela also went to Sweden to visit his old friend, Oliver Tambo, who had recently had a stroke. During one of their conversations, Tambo said to him, 'Nelson, you must now take over as president of the ANC. I have only been keeping the job warm for you.'

'No, Oliver,' responded Mandela. 'I can't do that. You have been a wonderful president all these years. I could never have done as good a job in exile as you did. The ANC is a democratic organisation. Let's wait for an election and do this thing properly.'

'Well, Nelson, I can't force you to take the job,' retorted Tambo, 'but I know you'll work hard for the organisation. And even though your title may be deputy president, people will treat you as if you are really the president of the ANC.'

It seemed that the unbanning of the political organisations and the release of Mandela and the others had lit a fire under South Africa. A huge pot was beginning to cook, and it looked like it might boil over. There were a lot of ingredients in the pot – moderate white people who were worried about losing their comfortable lifestyle, right-wing white nationalists who were determined not to accept majority rule, black radicals who thought that the only way to gain freedom was to drive the white people out of the country, Zulu nationalists who were set on having power in their own part of the country, and many others.

Whenever there was a bit of progress in the negotiations, there seemed to be another riot or massacre somewhere in the country. Often, there were reports that the police or the army were either helping the violence to happen, or not doing anything about it when they could. The pot got hotter.

Talks between the ANC and the government had begun in May 1990, just a few months after Mandela was released from prison. However, it was only in December 1991 that the official all-party negotiations, called the Convention for a Democratic South Africa, began. The negotiations continued for the next two years, with many interruptions caused by conflicts between various groups.

While the negotiations were slowly moving along, several things had happened to Mandela. He had been elected President of the ANC at its congress in July 1991.

Then, in April 1992, Mandela announced that he and Winnie were separating. There had been problems between them for some time. Winnie had had a difficult life in the years that Mandela was in prison. Her life continued to be stormy now that he was out of prison. She had recently been brought to trial for something she had done while Mandela was still in prison. She was found guilty of helping to kidnap several young boys whom she thought were police spies. One of the boys, Stompie Sepei, had been so badly beaten while in her care that he died later. That case was on appeal – waiting to be heard by a judge who would decide whether the first trial had been fair or not. She had her own group of friends, both political and social. She and Mandela did not agree at all on many issues and they were eventually divorced in 1996.

Mandela felt very bad about this situation. He thought that it was partially his fault that Winnie was having all these problems. If he had not been so committed to the struggle, and had not been in prison for so long, then they would have been able to lead a normal family life. He believed that if only he had been around, he would have been able to help her make the right decisions. Now it was too late.

In April 1993 Chris Hani was assassinated by a white right-winger outside his home in Boksburg, an East Rand suburb. Hani had been a popular leader of Umkhonto we Sizwe in exile, and was also the secretary-general of the South African Communist Party. He had the respect of the younger people of the country, many of whom thought that a violent solution was the only solution. He told them that they had to be disciplined, and they listened. There was a danger that Hani's death might lead to the beginning of a race war that would leave thousands dead.

When Mandela heard about the killing, he was visiting the home he had built in Qunu, where he had lived as a child. Because he was nearby, and believed in the traditional way of doing things, he went first to see Hani's father to offer his condolences. Then he flew to Johannesburg. That night, Mandela spoke to the nation on television. He appealed to the people to be calm. He begged them not to give in to an urge to take revenge. 'That will not honour Chris Hani's memory,' he said. 'That was not what Chris Hani stood for. As a soldier and as a freedom fighter he stood for discipline. To honour him you should also be disciplined.' Mandela said that people could express their grief by going to the funeral and taking part in demonstrations that the ANC would organise to protest Hani's killing and other violence.

It was the first time that Mandela, not De Klerk, had taken the lead in this way. He saw a serious problem and he dealt with it. He was the man who could and did control the people in a time of need. It was a turning point. From that time on, it seemed, the power of the government grew less – although there were still many problems to overcome – and the power of Mandela and the ANC grew.

Over the next few months, agreement was finally reached on a date for the first democratic elections, the size of the new parliament and the draft of an interim constitution* which gave equal rights to all the citizens of the country.

Towards the end of that year, Mandela was informed that he and FW de Klerk had jointly been awarded the Nobel Peace Prize. Only two other South Africans had received this award before – Albert Luthuli and Archbishop Desmond Tutu. Mandela was very proud.

The next few months were taken up with getting ready for the elections. Mandela, like many other people, spent a lot of time travelling around the country, asking people to vote for his political party. Madiba, as he was often called, was seen everywhere in his brightly-patterned silk shirts. He made speeches at meetings and rallies, and sometimes danced to the music that was played at these events. His slow dance became known as the Madiba jive.

ANC supporters carry an election poster for South Africa's first democratic election in April 1994

Finally, the great day came – 27 April 1994. Long lines of people waited for hours to vote, many of them for the first time in their lives. A few days later all the votes had been counted and the ANC had won 62,6% of the votes. It had been agreed during discussions about the Interim Constitution that the leader of the party that got the most votes would become the president of the country. Nelson Mandela, the former jailbird, was going to be President of South Africa.

President Mandela

13

On 10 May 1994, Nelson Mandela was sworn in as the president of the Republic of South Africa. Imagine starting a new career like this when you are 75 years old!

Thousands of South Africans gathered at the Union Buildings in Pretoria to watch the inauguration* ceremony. Hundreds of representatives from 170 different countries came to see the famous former prisoner become the head of his country. The new democracy had a new flag, a new national anthem – *Nkosi Sikelel' iAfrika* – and a new president.

The country and its people also had new hope that the future would be much better than the difficult and painful past. Building that future, though, was definitely not going to be easy. This was the beginning of another struggle. Mandela was trusted and admired by many people, and it was hoped that he would be able to win this new battle as well. During his speech at the inauguration, Mandela said, 'Out of the experience of an extraordinary human disaster that lasted too long, must be born a society of which all humanity will be proud.'

There were barriers to be overcome in the building of a new South Africa. Apartheid had had 46 years to put its structures in place. Before that there had been 300 years of colonial rule during which the foundations had been laid that had made apartheid possible. Even though there was now a democratic system of government where everybody could vote, this did not mean that there would instantly be a new way of life for everyone in the country. Poverty, illiteracy, unemployment and discrimination still existed.

A Government of National Unity (GNU) was formed. One of the main jobs of the new government was to get rid of the old structures of apartheid South Africa. For example, it created nine provinces and abolished the former homelands. It also adopted policies aimed at reducing the huge difference in wealth and living conditions between white and black South Africans.

There was another kind of problem, too. During the last few decades, people throughout the country had become very used to the idea of 'protest'. In the 1980s the ANC had called on the people to 'make South Africa ungovernable' and the people had responded. Many communities had stopped paying rent for their houses and money for their electricity to the local councils. There was a great deal of lawlessness in the country. Although there was now a new and democratic government and the need for this kind of protest was over, the attitude was not easy to change. It made the government's task of improving things in the country much harder.

The government started making changes. Houses were built, health care was made available to ordinary people, changes were being made in education. But the improvements were slow to come. People were sometimes impatient, thinking that they should have better housing and schooling and health care and jobs today, not tomorrow.

In his speech at the opening of parliament in February 1995, President Mandela called for an end to the crime and violence that were plaguing the country. 'Let me make it abundantly clear,' he said, 'that the small minority in our midst which wears the mask of anarchy* will meet its match in the government we lead.' He also asked the people to have patience. He said that their needs would be met, but that it would take time to overcome the centuries of neglect.

Apart from trying to improve the living conditions of the

majority of the people, Mandela had another goal – national reconciliation. He felt it was important to reassure white people that they would not suffer under the new government. He also believed that it was important for white South Africans to admit to the mistakes of the past so that there could be understanding and forgiveness.

With the first half of this – reassuring white people – Mandela was very successful. He made many gestures of goodwill. For example, he arranged a 'reconciliation lunch' to which he invited the wives and widows of former apartheid leaders and of black activists, hoping that they would learn to understand each other better. 'These are the wives of the heroes of both sides,' he said.

He also invited to lunch Percy Yutar, the prosecutor in the Rivonia Trial. After the judge sentenced the group to life imprisonment, Yutar had said he was disappointed that they would not be hanged. He was amazed not only that he was invited to lunch with the President, but that Mandela showed no hatred towards him. Afterwards, Yutar said to a reporter, 'I wonder in what other country of the world you would have the head of the government inviting someone to lunch who prosecuted him 30 years ago. It shows the great humility of this saintly man.'

One other important way in which Mandela reassured white South Africans had to do with the rugby World Cup competition in 1995. During the 1980s, when the ANC had called for sanctions and boycotts against the country, South Africa's teams were banned from participating in international contests. This was a great blow to white South African sports lovers. After Mandela was released from prison, the world again welcomed South African sportsmen and women to big competitions, and the country was delighted. The rugby World Cup was the first big rugby competition that they had been able to participate in for a long time. Mandela made a point of meeting with the rugby team. During the final game, held in Johannesburg, he even came to the stadium wearing a rugby jersey with the team captain's number on it. The crowd loved it. 'NEL-SON! NEL-SON! NEL-SON!' they chanted. When the South African team won, thousands of people, black and white, celebrated throughout the country. It brought the people of the country closer together.

The second part of the government's strategy of reconciliation involved the setting up of a Truth and Reconciliation Commission (TRC). The TRC could call witnesses and hold hearings into the activities of individuals during the apartheid regime. The idea was that those who freely admitted their crimes against their fellow South Africans and who could show a political motive, could be pardoned. If they were not granted amnesty*, they could be prosecuted by the courts. Thousands of people, witnesses and accused alike, were heard during various sessions of the TRC throughout the country. Some terrible stories were told. Parents heard how their children had been brutally tortured. Details were recounted about bombings, stabbings, poisonings and kidnappings. Many white people inside the country, and many people in other countries, were amazed at the horrific stories that were told during these hearings. Before this they had not realised how bad apartheid had been, and the awful things that had been done to people in the name of the apartheid government. Now the whole world was finding out. Although it was very painful to relive these memories, in a way the process was a release valve. It often helped the victims and their families to hear the details and sometimes the apologies of the men who had done these things. On the whole, it was a tool of reconciliation.

Although Mandela was working hard for the country, he was not a saint; nor was he perfect. He had to face the results of some bad judgements that he made. Mandela was very loyal to his friends, even when they got into trouble. He often didn't want to believe that they had done wrong. Also, because of his long time in prison, he wasn't always aware of the entire background of a situation. One example of this kind of thing was his relationship with President Suharto of Indonesia. During one of his tours shortly after being released from prison, Mandela had visited Indonesia and was very well received by Suharto. Mandela was so impressed by Suharto's kindness and wealth that he asked for and received $10 million for the ANC to use in its election campaign.

There was a lot of criticism about this, because in 1976 Suharto had invaded East Timor, a former colony of Portugal. He had imprisoned the leader of the East Timorese liberation movement, Jose Xanana Gusmao, and over the years Suharto's soldiers had killed thousands of people in East Timor. Many people thought that Mandela shouldn't have anything to do with this ruler who abused human rights so badly. Mandela, though, continued the relationship and in 1997, when Suharto was visiting South Africa, even presented him with the Order of Good Hope, South Africa's most important medal. Some said that Mandela continued to talk to Suharto because he hoped to influence him to release Gusmao and negotiate the freedom of East Timor. Others said that Mandela was selling his honour for money.

Although Mandela could live in the president's official residences in Cape Town and Pretoria, he had bought a house of his own in Johannesburg where he lived with some of his grandchildren. He felt life was simpler here than in the impressive surroundings of the official residences. Out of the habit of many years in prison, Mandela continued to make his own bed every morning, even though he was now President of the country. He donated one third of his salary to the Nelson Mandela Children's Fund, a charity that he had established to help children in need. He travelled around the country asking business people and others for help for the children. Many schools and clinics were built in poor areas through this fund.

Mandela made it clear to everyone that while he would

complete his five-year term of office as president, he would not serve another. 'I will be too old to do a proper job of running the country after that,' he said. Even in his first term, he left much of the day-to-day work of running the country to his deputy presidents, Thabo Mbeki and FW de Klerk. It was generally understood that Mandela favoured Mbeki as the next president of the ANC and of the country, and that he was being prepared for these positions.

In 1997 it became clear to the country that Mandela had a special new friend. He was spending more and more time with Graça Machel, the widow of the first president of Mozambique, Samora Machel. She accompanied him on many occasions, often serving as his hostess and official companion. She made him smile. He seemed to be a happier and more relaxed man when he was with her. Finally, Mandela convinced her to marry him and they became husband and wife on his 80th birthday, 18 July 1998. Although

Nelson and Graça on the Blue Train in September 1997

she kept her own name, South Africa had a new First Lady. Mandela continued to travel the world, making new friends for the country. One of the reasons that there had been so much faith in the new democracy was certainly Nelson Mandela. He soothed the worries of the world, and assured many countries that there would be stability in South Africa. As the time for South Africa's second democratic elections neared, Mandela toured many countries, this time saying goodbye. It would be his last trip as president.

On 2 June 1999, the country went to the polls, and again the ANC won a huge victory. Thabo Mbeki was sworn in as President of South Africa on 16 June 1999. Although Mandela was now the former president, it was hard to think of him that way. During the celebrations after Mbeki's inauguration as president, Mandela was referred to as 'President Mandela' more than once!

Mandela was often asked what he would do when he retired. To this question he would usually reply that he would do the things that he had not had time to do before – spend time with his children and grandchildren, read and write his memoirs.

This man who had come out of prison not bitter, not hating, but willing and ready to work for a peaceful future for his country, had given more than 50 years of his life to the struggle for liberation. Even as he was looking forward to a well-earned rest, he said, 'I am a loyal and disciplined member of the African National Congress. I will always be ready to answer its call.'

Learn new words

amnesty: pardon for an offence committed. (see page 68)

anarchy: social and political disorder. (see page 66)

articled clerk: an 'apprentice' lawyer. (see page 13)

assegai: a spear. (see page 5)

banned: affected by a government banning order. (see page 20)

banning order: an order of the government which prevented the banned person from taking part in political activities. Sometimes a banning order would say the person could not go outside a certain area, or that he or she could not be in the company of more than one person at a time. (see page 23)

censored: checked by the authorities. Information about forbidden topics was either cut out or blacked out. (see page 45)

circumcision: cutting off the foreskin of the penis, sometimes as part of a ceremony. (see page 5)

clandestinely: secretly. (see page 32)

colonialism: a system where strong countries control weaker ones, often exploiting them for economic gain. (see page 16)

communist: a believer in communism. Communism is a political philosophy that says that all factories, mines, shops and other businesses should be owned by the state instead of by individuals, and that everyone should share equally in the country's wealth. (see page 13)

confiscated: taken away by an authority as a punishment. (see page 2)

consensus: general agreement on an issue. (see page 5)

efficacy: effectiveness. (see page 35)

escalating: growing in size or strength. (see page 53)

freelance: working for oneself and not for an employer. (see page 29)

galvanise: shock into action. (see page 17)

heifer: a young cow that has not yet had a calf. (see page 6)

inauguration: a ceremony to introduce the new president. (see page 65)

incriminating: something which could be used as evidence of guilt. (see page 31)

indictment: a formal accusation made at the beginning of a court case. (see page 29)

induna: on the mines, an African foreman in charge of African workers. (see page 11)

interim constitution: a temporary constitution, which was agreed on by participants in the multi-party talks, and which would be presented to the new parliament after the election to be agreed on or changed. (see page 63)

intimidate: frighten. (see page 40)

pass laws: laws which said that Africans had to carry a pass book. The book had to be stamped by the local authority and signed by the person's employer. If a person was not carrying his or her pass book, or if it was not in order, he or she could be arrested. (see page 14)

passive resistance: resisting by peaceful means. (see page 18)

prophetic: having the ability to tell what will happen in the future. (see page 20)

prosecutor: a person who brings a criminal charge against someone in a court of law. (see page 27)

ratify: to confirm or accept. (see page 25)

referendum: a vote on a single issue. (see page 34)

regent: someone who rules instead of the heir to the throne until the heir is old enough to rule for himself or herself. (see page 4)

repeal: to abolish a law. (see page 23)

reprieve: an official order to stop the punishment of a prisoner. (see page 42)

statutory communism: communism as defined by an Act of Parliament, not necessarily the political philosophy described above. (see page 22)

Special Branch: a section of the former South African police force whose task it was to observe and investigate political events and political people in the country, especially those who were believed to be acting against the government. (see page 36)

treason: plotting to overthrow the state. (see page 26)

white supremacy: a belief of white people that they were better than people of other races, and therefore had the right to rule over them. (see page 19)

Activities

1 **Choose the correct answer**

(a) Nelson Mandela refused to serve on the Students' Representative Council (SRC) during his second year at university because
(i) black students could not vote
(ii) the majority of students had not voted
(iii) his friends did not want him to

(b) The ANC Youth League was formed in 1944 to
(i) pressurise ANC leadership to oppose the government more actively
(ii) promote communism
(iii) encourage passive resistance

(c) The Freedom Charter was a document that
(i) reflected the wishes of ANC members only
(ii) reflected the wishes of people who supported the government
(iii) promised equality for all South Africans

(d) In 1963, Umkhonto we Sizwe was established
(i) as an army in opposition to the ANC
(ii) to put pressure on the government through sabotage
(iii) as a passive resistance movement

(e) On 11 February 1990, Nelson Mandela was released from prison after
    (i)   20 years
    (ii) 17 years
    (iii) 27 years

2 Group discussion

(a) The Sharpeville massacre was a turning point in South African history. Why do you think the police reacted the way they did? Why were South Africa and the rest of the world so shocked by this? What chain of events took place afterwards that resulted in Mandela's arrest on charges of treason?

(b) In his autobiography, Mandela wrote that 'the challenge for every prisoner . . . is how to survive prison intact, how to emerge from prison un-diminished . . .'
Think about the challenges Mandela faced in prison. Imagine how you would feel if you were in this position. In groups, discuss ways in which you could try to overcome the hardships.

3 Discuss, argue and debate

Divide the class into two groups. Imagine that it is 1961. Hold a debate in which one group argues for non-violent passive resistance and the other group argues for an armed struggle. Afterwards, make a poster that reflects the most important points of both sides of the debate.

More books about the life and times of Nelson Mandela

Benson, M. 1986. *Nelson Mandela: The Man and the Movement.* London: Penguin.

Clark, S. (ed.) 1993. *Nelson Mandela Speaks: Forging a Democratic Non-racial South Africa.* Cape Town: David Philip.

Daniel, J. and B. Pogrund. 1992. *Nelson Mandela.* Milwaukee: Gareth Stevens Children's Books.

Green, P. and P. Wilhelm. 1994. A beacon for the world. *Leadership.* 13(2):8–18.

Gregory, J. 1995. *Goodbye Bafana. Nelson Mandela: My Prisoner, My Friend.* London: Headline Book Publishing.

Johns, S. and R.H. Davis Jr. 1991. *Mandela, Tambo and the African National Congress. The Struggle Against Apartheid, 1948–1990.* Oxford: Oxford University Press.

Mandela, N.R. 1994. *Long Walk to Freedom.* Johannesburg: Macdonald Purnell.

Meer, F. Undated. *Higher than Hope, Nelson Mandela's Biography on his 70th Birthday.* Durban: Institute for Black Research, Madiba Publishers.

Meredith, M. 1997. *Nelson Mandela. A Biography.* London: Penguin.

Sampson, A. 1999. *Mandela. The Authorised Biography.* London and Johannesburg: HarperCollins and Jonathan Ball.

Schadeberg, J. (ed.) 1990. *Nelson Mandela and the Rise of the ANC.* Parklands: Jonathan Ball and Ad. Donker.